SLEEP

Lesley Newson

Contents

SCIENCE MYSTERIES

A&C BLACK · LONDON

An overnight journey

A night's sleep is like a mysterious journey. You can remember going to bed and you may remember feeling sleepy, but no one can remember falling asleep. When you start to wake up, you may have clear memories of things that you have just been dreaming about. They may have been exciting, frightening, strange or silly. They often seem very clear and real until your mind gets used to the idea of being awake.

This is a painting of the Bible story of Jacob's dream. As the story illustrates, dreaming is a safe and effortless way of having the most amazing experiences. But what do the experiences mean?

Most people have trouble with sleep at some time in their lives. You may not be able to get to sleep on some nights, or you may feel very sleepy when you want to stay awake during the day. While you're asleep you may have horrible nightmares. Your body may do things you don't want it to do; you may talk, get out of bed and walk around, or wet the bed while you are asleep. No one really knows why these things happen.

Most of the time, when people sleep, they lie perfectly still. Their faces are calm. Their eyes are closed. Then suddenly, they move. The face may twist into a sort of a smile or frown or something in between. The body may turn over or just flop about. Then all is calm again.

There is a great deal we don't know about sleep. People spend about a third of their lives asleep and yet no one really knows what sleep is for.

For thousands of years, people have been wondering why they have to sleep and why they have dreams. This book is about what people have discovered about sleep and the ideas they have had. No one knows which ideas are right and the search is still going on for more clues.

Many artists have seen a special beauty in the peaceful form of a person sleeping. This sculpture of a sleeping slave boy was made in Egypt about 2000 years ago.

What do we dream about?

In almost all dreams, at least one other person known to the dreamer makes an appearance.

We seldom bother to dream about the things we do as part of our daily routine, such as brushing our teeth or washing the dishes. On the other hand, our dreams are not usually bizarre and fantastic either, although it's those we remember best.

In about a third of dreams, the dreamer is active in some way and not just observing.

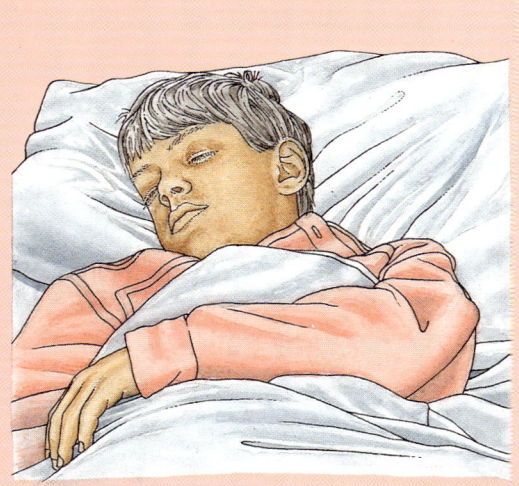

Physical work is almost always done without effort in dreams.

In another third, the dreamer is moving.

Crazy for sleep?

One way to find out clues about why we need sleep is to stay awake and see what happens. Doctors and scientists use sleep deprivation experiments to test how the body and brain react as people go longer and longer without sleep. The people taking part in these experiments are prevented from dropping off to sleep, even for a few seconds.

Scientists' tests show that people who have been deprived of one night's sleep are usually able to carry on and do things just as well as people who have slept normally. With every sleepless night that follows, the volunteers find it harder and harder to think clearly and remember. They also become less able to control their bodies.

All of these problems are caused by the brain not working well. However, the rest of the body remains basically healthy, even after several nights without sleep. But tests have shown that the body does change. The concentration of some of its chemicals alters and and the body temperature of some volunteers drops to as much as a degree below normal. People taking part in sleep deprivation experiments feel very hungry and eat much more than they usually do.

Case study: Randy Gardener

In 1964 in California, a record-breaking sleep deprivation experiment was begun as a science project by Randy Gardener, a seventeen-year-old schoolboy. Until then, the longest anyone had stayed awake was 260 hours. Randy planned to stay awake for 264 hours, or 11 days. Doctors and scientists researching into sleep at a nearby hospital monitored Randy during the experiment.

After Randy's first night without sleep, his eyes became so tired, he could no longer watch television. After a second sleepless night, Randy started to become quite moody and his movements were more clumsy. His speech was slightly slurred and he had trouble with easy tongue twisters.

After a third night without sleep, Randy was more bad tempered, couldn't concentrate and had gaps in his memory. He said he could see a fog around streetlights and had a feeling of a tight band around his head.

Tests show that going without sleep causes changes in the levels of certain chemicals in the blood, but the body still appears to be basically healthy.

He also started imagining things. He believed he was a great football player for a while and mistook a street sign for a person.

By day nine, Randy's memory was so bad, he often couldn't talk sensibly. He forgot what he was going to say halfway through sentences and his speech was only a mumble.

Randy Gardener did manage to stay awake for the eleven days and this is still a world record.

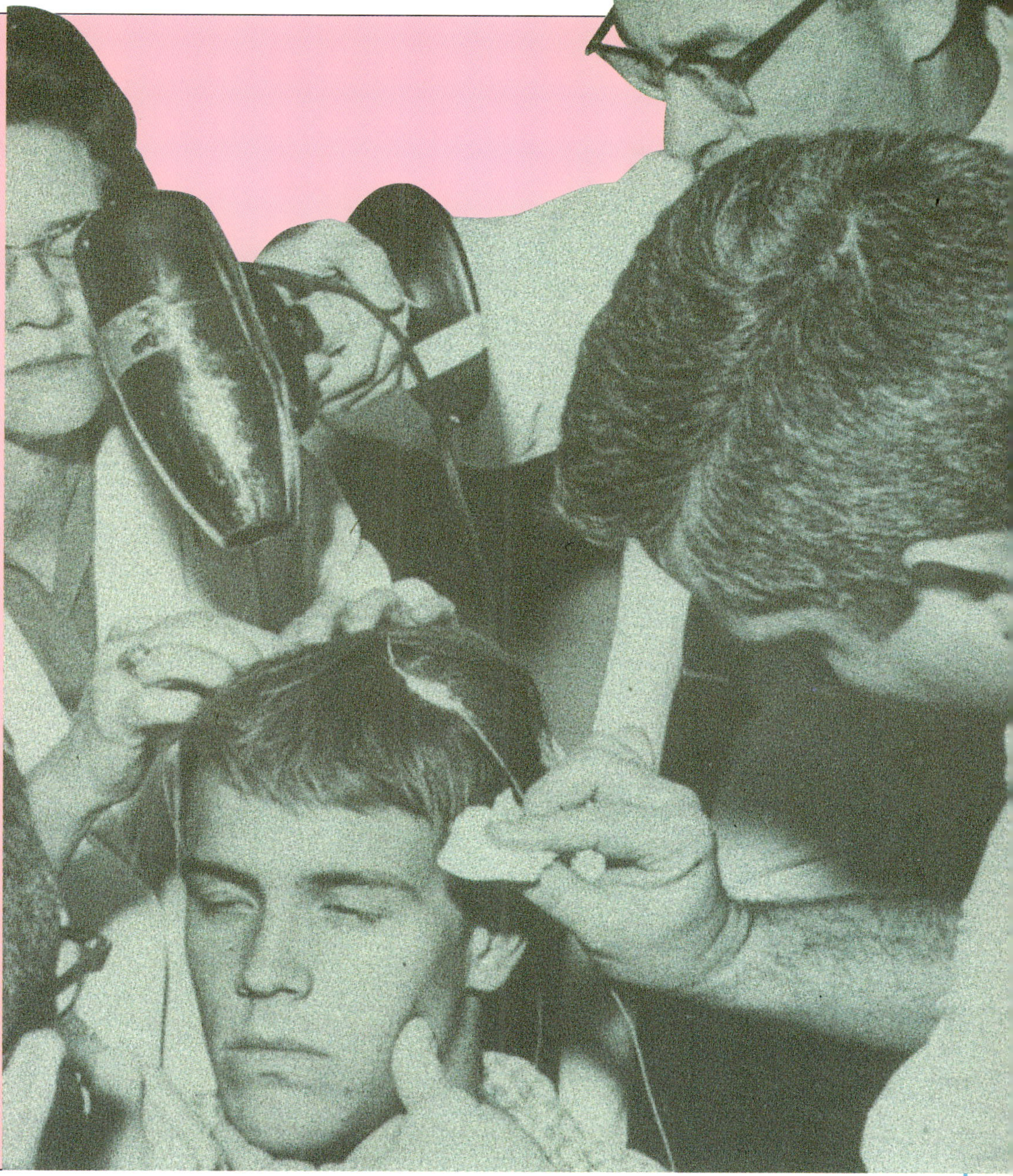

This photograph of Randy Gardener was taken at the end of his eleven days without sleep. The scientists are preparing to monitor his brain while he sleeps.

Sleep deprivation experiments have shown that, after only one good night's sleep, the volunteers can think and behave more or less as normal, even after previously going without sleep for more than a week. What these experiments don't explain is why going without sleep causes changes to the body and brain. What is it about sleep that keeps the body and brain working well? What is going on inside the brain while we sleep?

Patients who attend sleep clinics for help with sleep problems are asked to fill in a questionnaire about themselves. Personality tests are one of a range of tests which doctors can use to judge how a person's brain is functioning. Tests show that going without sleep can have a severe effect on how well the brain works.

A chance to dream?

Something important must be happening to us when we sleep, but what? Our dreams are all we can ever remember about the time we have spent asleep. Perhaps we need to sleep in order to have dreams.

There is evidence that, even before the beginning of recorded history, human beings have been fascinated by their dreams and have wondered about their meaning.

In the 1800s, explorers visited tribes in Australia, Siberia, South America and many other parts of the world. The members of these tribes had no experience of life outside the small area where they lived. The ideas these people expressed may have changed little from the beliefs held by human communities who lived before the beginning of recorded history.

Some dogs move their legs and give little barks while they sleep. Are they dreaming about chasing something or running away from something?

Dreams were very important to many of these tribes, and the explorers were amazed to find that different peoples often told remarkably similar stories about their dreams. People living on the edge of Hudson Bay in Canada were found to have similar beliefs to people living in the Malaysian jungle of South East Asia. Both peoples believed that their spirits left their bodies during sleep and travelled in a dream world.

To many of the members of these tribes, the memories of their dreams were just as real and important as the memories of things that happened to them when they were awake.

Warriors belonging to some Native American tribes believed that they met their guardian spirits in their dreams. On waking, they made objects such as this shield cover, which they decorated with images remembered from their dreams.

The first written evidence of people's thoughts about dreams comes from the early civilizations of Greece, Egypt, India and Babylon. Ancient writings from 3000 years ago show that people of this time believed dreams to be very important. They thought that gods or spirits could visit people in their dreams and give them messages. The messages could be about the future, they could contain advice to sick people to help them get better, or they could just help the dreamer to become more wise.

These are the remains of a temple to the Greek god of medicine. About 3000 years ago in Greece, sick people would spend the night in the temple. The next morning they would tell their dreams to the priests and priestesses who would explain the medical advice contained in the dreams.

The Bible tells of important messages that came to people in dreams. In one Old Testament story, God helps Joseph, a prisoner in Egypt, interpret the dreams of the Pharoah.

In one dream, seven fat cows are eaten by seven thin cows. In the other, seven plump stalks of wheat are eaten by seven thin stalks. Joseph explains that the dreams contain messages about the future. They mean that there will be very good harvests for the next seven years, but in the following seven years the harvests will be very bad. Joseph warns the Pharoah to save food from the good harvests – otherwise his people will starve when the harvests are bad.

At the beginning of the twentieth century, many people believed that talking about dreams could help to cure illness. At this time, the ideas of Sigmund Freud were helping to change the way people thought about the human mind and about why people become mentally ill.

Sigmund Freud

Freud, an Austrian doctor who lived from 1856 to 1939, believed that people can be troubled by thoughts and memories that they have hidden, even from themselves. He invented a treatment for mental illness, called psychoanalysis, which aimed to help people discover and face up to these troublesome thoughts. Freud believed that we dream about the things we wish we could do. He thought that dreams, even silly ones, can contain clues to a person's hidden wishes.

Many of Freud's patients lay on this couch in his consulting room. Freud believed that relaxed patients would be more likely to reveal clues about their problems. He spent many hours with his patients, trying to work out the meaning of their dreams.

Carl Jung

Carl Jung, a Swiss psychiatrist who lived from 1875 to 1961, worked with Freud for some time. Jung agreed that dreams could be a route to discovering the thoughts and wishes which are stored in the 'unconscious', the part of the mind which is hidden by our conscious, waking thoughts.

Jung thought that during dreams, the unconscious mind helps the dreamer to sort out problems by allowing the dreamer to see things from different angles. For Jung, dreams were not just a way of helping to cure mentally ill people; he thought that they were the human mind's way of keeping itself healthy.

Over the centuries, many people have taken advantage of other people's need to understand their dreams. These 'dream explainers' charged people money for the interpretations they had fabricated.

When the Islamic prophet Muhammad lived in Arabia between the years 570 and 632 AD, many people visited dream explainers, whose claims to be able to interpret the messages contained within dreams made them powerful and rich. Muhammad saw that this was not helping his people, and said that the followers of the Muslim religion must not look for messages or advice from dreams.

It's certainly true that most people feel better after a good night's sleep. But is this because their dreams make problems seem easier to handle or is it just because they aren't tired any more? Is there a way to explore the importance of dreams scientifically?

One way to discover clues about the effect of dreaming on the human mind is to prevent a group of people from dreaming and compare them to people who are allowed to dream normally. Several groups of scientists have tried to do this by waking people when they seem to be about to start dreaming. It isn't possible to know for sure when a sleeper is dreaming, but scientists can tell when a person is most likely

to be having vivid dreams (see page 12). Most people taking part in these experiments did show some changes. They often seemed to be quieter than usual, a bit more confused and worried. But this does not really tell us anything about what dreams may be doing. Despite the work of scientists and philosophers, the reasons why we dream are still a mystery.

Looking for messages in dreams may have led to the Emperor Montezuma's downfall. In 1520 this powerful leader of the Aztecs in Mexico was easily defeated by the forces of Spain. Many historians think that Montezuma did not put up a fight against the Spanish because he believed he had foreseen his defeat at their hands.

Brainwaves

In the 1920s, a German doctor called Hans Berger discovered that special sensors glued to the skin on top of the head could pick up tiny electrical changes happening in the brain. When the signal from the sensors is drawn on a graph, it looks like this:

This is a recording of only 20 seconds of signals from the brain. The spiky wavy line on the graph was given the nickname 'brainwaves', but its proper name is electroencephalogram, or EEG for short.

The invention of the electroencephalogram gave scientists a way of recording activity inside the brain. Using EEG recordings to learn about the brain is a bit like trying to find out about an underground railway by listening with your ear to the ground above. It can't possibly tell you what is really going on but it can allow you to detect patterns. With your ear to the ground above an underground railway, for example, you would hear different patterns of noises depending on the time of day. During the morning and evening rush hours, the rumbling noises would occur more often.

Experiments have shown that the brain is made up of billions of special cells that carry and pass on tiny electrical signals. The EEG detects patterns in the work of the brain cells. The EEG showed scientists that while we sleep, our brain cells work to different patterns, depending on which stage of sleep we have reached.

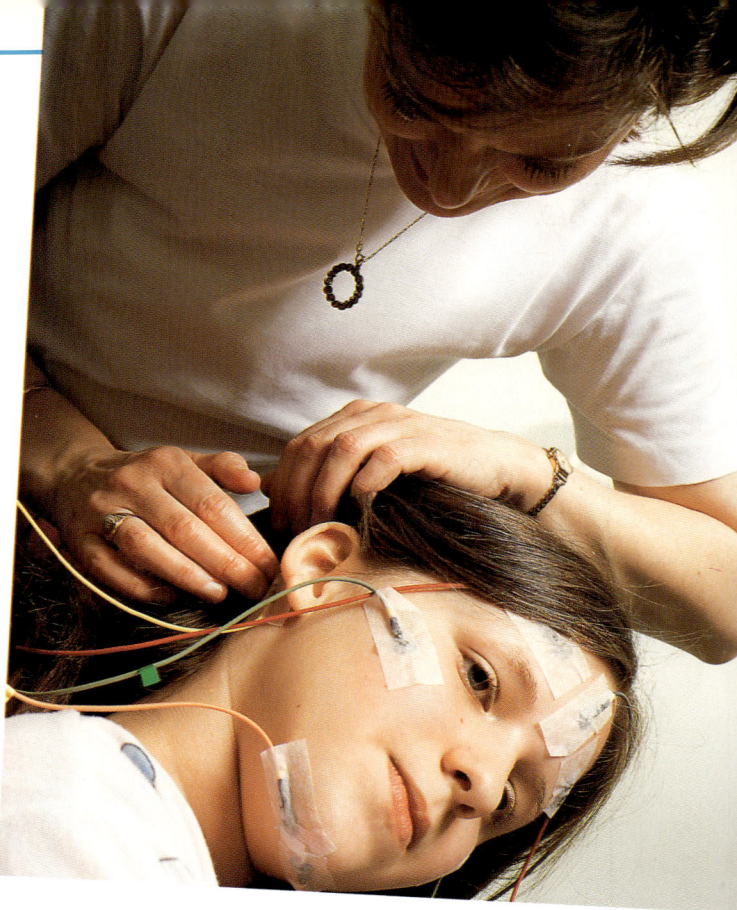

To record the EEG, sensors called 'electrodes' are glued to the skin.

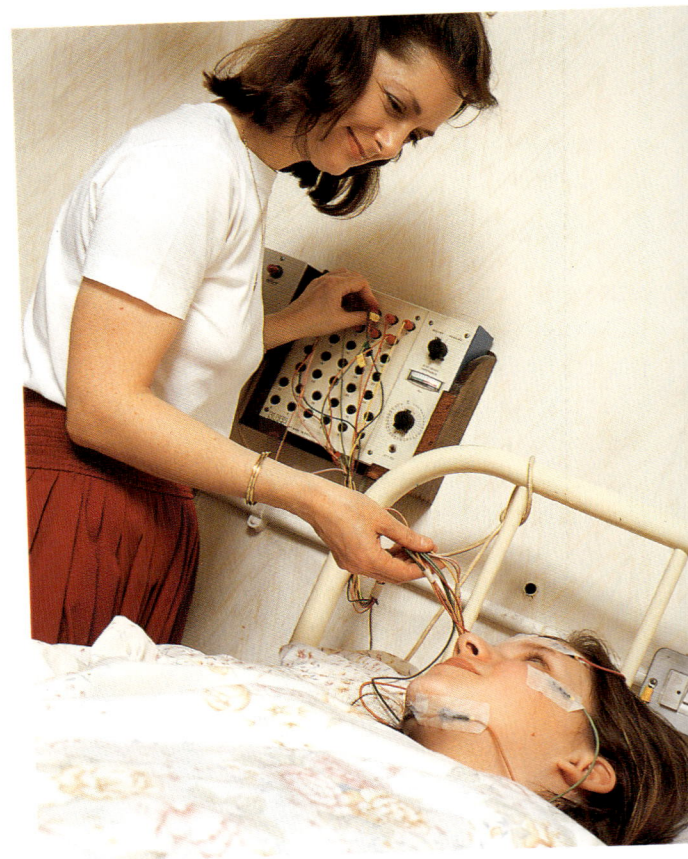

It's difficult to sleep while wearing electrodes, but not impossible.

If you were having your brainwaves recorded now, the EEG would look like this:

At bedtime when you start dropping off to sleep, the pattern of waves changes slightly:

It would be very easy to wake you up during this stage of sleep. If something did wake you, you would probably say that you hadn't been asleep. Scientists call this Stage One Sleep.

A few minutes later, if you aren't woken up, you slip down into Stage Two Sleep and your EEG looks like this:

Your EEG keeps slowly changing and after a few more minutes it begins to look like this:

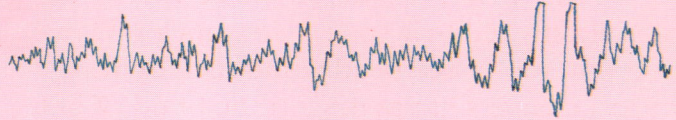

This is called Stage Three Sleep. People in this stage of sleep are so deeply asleep that noises and people walking into the room do not usually wake them.

Soon you enter the deepest stage of sleep, Stage Four Sleep, when your EEG looks like this:

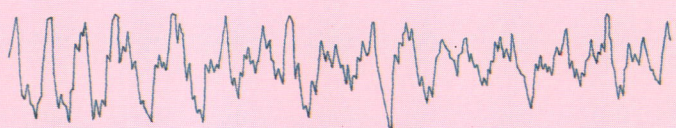

This is also called Slow Wave Sleep, because the rhythm of the brainwaves is so much slower.

Scientists have recorded the nightly EEG changes of many thousands of people who are asleep and have found that almost everyone follows the same pattern of sleep stages. Once people reach Stage Four Sleep, they stay in that stage for 20 minutes or so, depending on how tired they are. Then they start to sleep more lightly. Their EEG shows them going back through stages three, two and one. Then the pattern of waves becomes similar to the EEG of an awake person.

In the next room, the tiny electrical changes detected by the electrodes are recorded as a jagged line.

The changing brainwaves show that a normal night's sleep has several cycles of light sleep, deep sleep, light sleep and periods of sleep when the brain appears to be awake. Each sleep cycle is about an hour and a half long. As the night goes on, people spend less time sleeping deeply and more time with a brainwave pattern which is similar to the awake pattern.

Why do we sometimes have 'awake' brainwaves when we are sound asleep? In 1952, sleep researcher Nathaniel Kleitman at the University of Chicago in the United States, noticed something which caused scientists to take a special interest in this stage of sleep.

Dr Kleitman called this stage of sleep 'Rapid Eye Movement' (or REM) sleep. He noticed that when people are in REM sleep, they never turn over or move. The body may give a little twitch, but otherwise it remains still. When Dr Kleitman woke people up during a period of REM sleep, they almost always said that they were in the middle of a dream. People who were woken up during other sleep stages sometimes reported dreams and often said that they had been thinking about something, but the dreams of REM sleep were the most colourful and exciting.

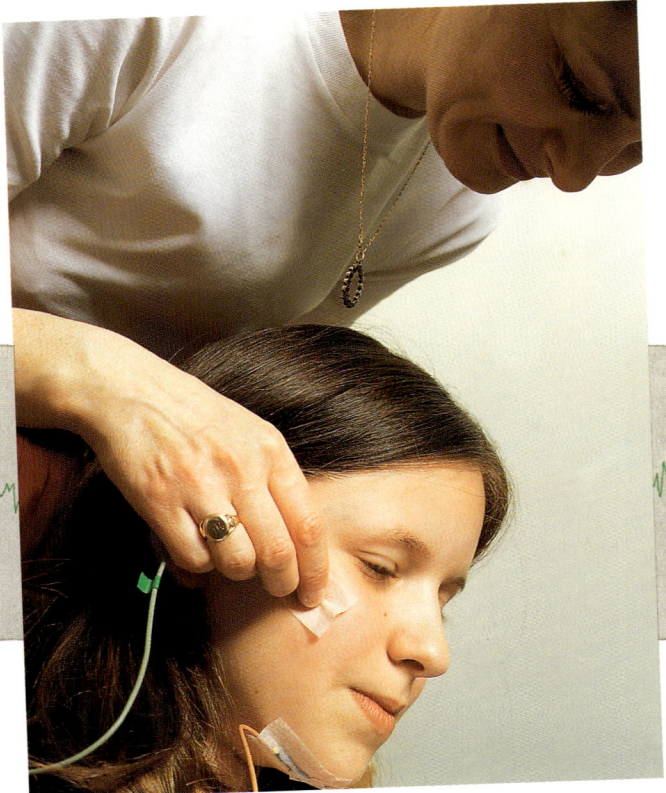

Dr Kleitman made his discovery by accident when he was investigating the way people's eyes begin to roll as they drop off to sleep. The rolling stops once a person falls more deeply asleep and the eyes become still. But when sleep becomes lighter and the brainwaves begin to show a more 'awake' pattern, the eyes start to move again.

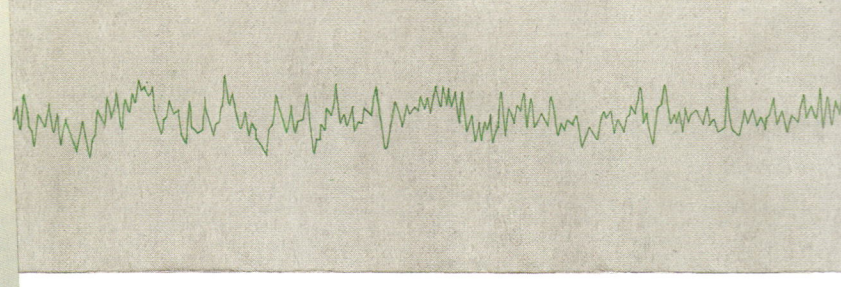

Detectors placed beside the eyes show that when a person is in REM sleep, their eyeballs dart around underneath their closed eyelids.

Many artists have tried to create pictures of what is happening in the mind of a dreamer.
This picture, called The Artist's Dream, _is by the British painter Edward Henry Corbould (1815-1905)._

During REM sleep, the brain seems to behave like an awake brain, but with one important difference. When you are awake, your brain is sending signals to the rest of your body, telling your muscles to move. But as you start to dream, these signals are prevented from travelling out of your brain.

This means that if you have a dream about riding a bicycle, your brain will be sending out signals telling your legs to pedal and your arms to steer, but the signals will never reach your arms and legs. You will keep lying perfectly still. If your brain didn't become disconnected in this way, you would act out your dreams, performing bizarre and possibly dangerous movements.

Many people report having dreams where they feel rooted to the spot. However much they try to move, they can't. It's most likely people experience this sensation just before they wake up. By the time they have woken up properly, their dreams have ended and their brains have been reconnected to their muscles so that they can move again.

Animal sleep

Every mammal and bird spends some of its time asleep. Other kinds of animals seem to need sleep too, but their sleeping habits are more difficult to work out.

For instance, how can you tell when a fish is asleep? Fish don't have eyelids and they can't close their eyes. Even so, many fish do seem to spend some time each day perfectly still as if they are asleep. So do reptiles, amphibians and insects.

Even though the trunk fish can't close its eyes, it does appear to be asleep. A diver can swim right up close to the fish and it won't move.

If animals are prevented from having their normal rest time, even simple animals such as cockroaches will take a longer rest period later, as if they are catching up on their sleep.

Mammals differ enormously in their sleeping habits because their sleep has to fit into their lifestyle. Some sleep by day, some by night. Some have one long sleep each day; others have several shorter sleeping times.

Mammals vary in the number of hours they spend asleep each day:

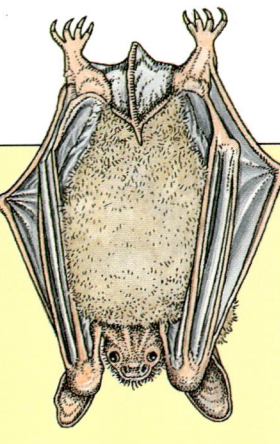

bat 20

mouse 13

mole 8-9

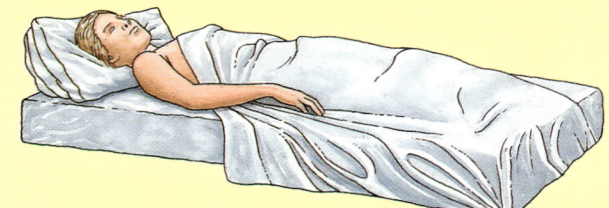

human 7-8

cow, horse, elephant 3

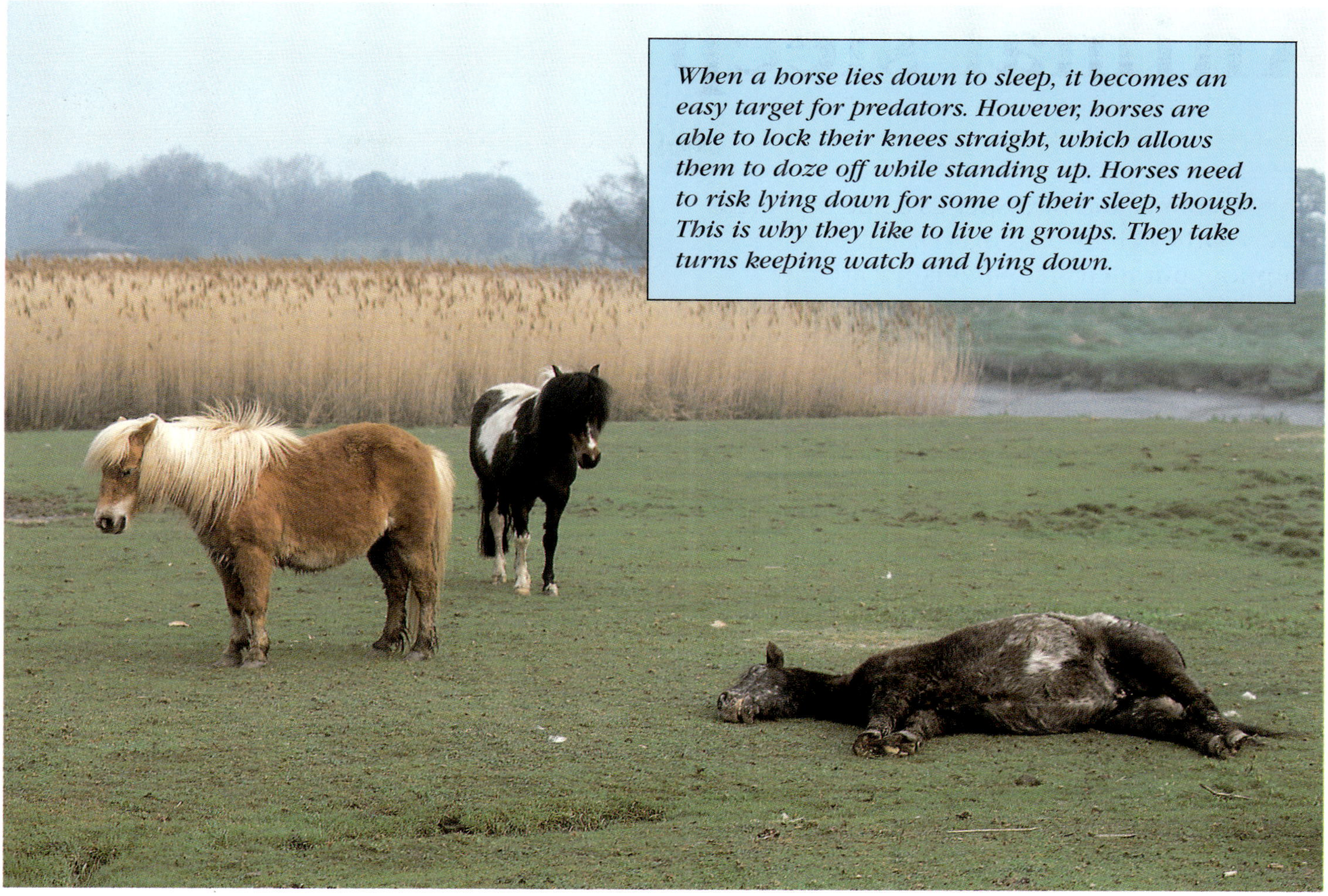

When a horse lies down to sleep, it becomes an easy target for predators. However, horses are able to lock their knees straight, which allows them to doze off while standing up. Horses need to risk lying down for some of their sleep, though. This is why they like to live in groups. They take turns keeping watch and lying down.

Pet dogs and cats wake up several times during the night and these pets usually have several naps during the day. This is partly because they are so well looked after. If they lived in the wild, they wouldn't have such a warm, comfortable and safe place to sleep. They would have less time to sleep because they would have to hunt for food.

At times when food is scarce, some mammals and birds go into a very deep sleep, or torpor, for several days or weeks. While these animals sleep, all their body functions become slower. This saves energy so their store of fat and food can last until times are better.

Most kinds of animals just slow down a little and their body temperature only drops a few degrees but others, such as weasels, hamsters, dormice, hedgehogs and some forms of bats, go into true hibernation. Their body temperature may drop to nearly freezing and they breathe only a few times a minute.

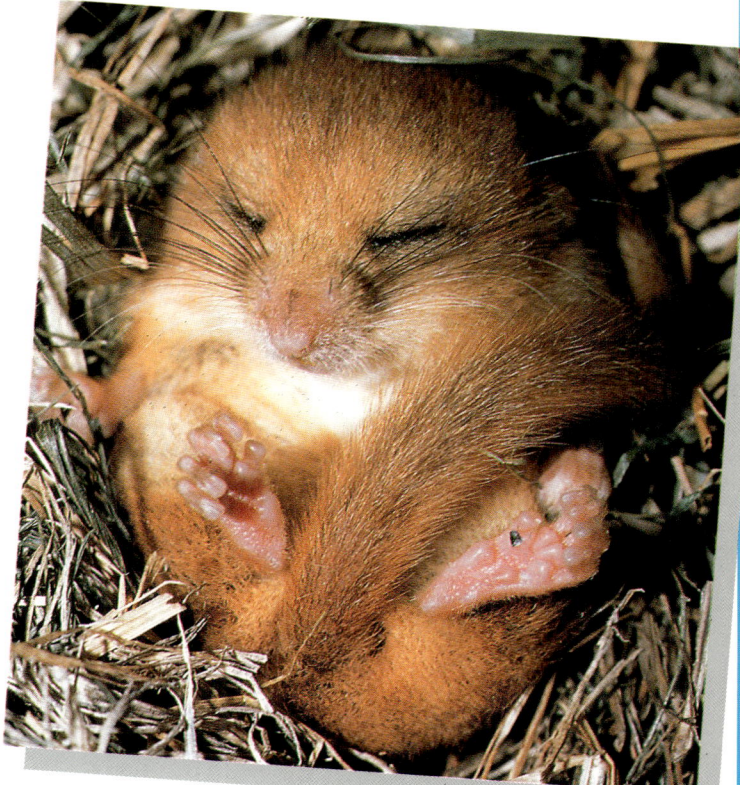

While this dormouse is in true hibernation, it seems almost dead.

Even though the sleeping habits of many animals may be very different from our own, some animals do share similarities with humans. The brainwaves of monkeys and apes look almost identical to human brainwaves. The patterns change as they sleep to show that they also have four stages of sleep and a time of Rapid Eye Movement (REM) sleep when they probably dream.

Other mammals have a similar, if simpler, pattern of light and deep sleep, but every mammal that has been tested has an EEG pattern of deep, slow, rhythmic waves when they are deeply asleep, and almost all have periods of REM sleep. While a mammal is in REM sleep, its brain signals are disconnected from the rest of its body just as happens during human REM sleep.

Studying animal sleep shows us that sleep is important to them just as it is to us, and that different animals have different ways of taking the sleep they need. What the studies have not shown, is why sleep is so important.

Dolphins are probably the strangest sleepers. They have to keep swimming up to the surface to breathe in air, so they are never able to relax as completely as other mammals.

Bottle-nosed dolphins and porpoises solve this problem by half-sleeping. The left hand side of the brain goes to sleep while the right hand side stays awake. Then they swap over. They go on changing shifts like this every two hours or so throughout the night.

Hibernation

In hibernating animals, it is difficult to detect any brainwave activity most of the time. However, every few weeks these animals emerge from hibernation for a couple of hours without waking up. The brainwaves change to show that the animals spend these hours asleep, before going back into hibernation.

Irene Tobler of the University of Zurich, who has studied the sleep of many animals, says that these findings are significant: 'Hibernating isn't the same as sleeping and I think these animals come out of hibernation in order to sleep. We are still working to discover why animals have to sleep.'

How much sleep do we need?

Do you jump out of bed feeling rested in the morning or do you take a while to wake up?

Do you have to be woken up in time to get ready for school or work?

In the early 1970s, American sleep researchers Wilse Webb and Harmon Agnew asked a thousand young adults these questions. They found that less than a third of the people they interviewed felt completely rested after a night's sleep. About a third reported that they couldn't wake up at the right time without an alarm clock. Does this mean that most people don't get enough sleep?

The amount of time people spend asleep depends partly on their age. Like all young animals, newborn humans spend most of the day asleep. As they grow older, they spend less and less time sleeping. Young adults sleep for about seven and a half hours on average. When people become elderly, many have trouble sticking to the sleeping schedule of their younger days. They may have several naps during the day and evening but not sleep very well at night.

Within each age group, there are people who sleep much more or much less than average. In the 1970s scientists in Switzerland followed the changes in sleeping behaviour of 320 children as they grew up. The amount of time they spent sleeping varied enormously between children. At the age of five, for example, the number of hours the children spent asleep varied from eight to fifteen hours a night.

There are some famous examples of non-average sleepers.

Napoleon, the French general who conquered almost all of Europe in the early 19th Century, went to bed between 10 pm and midnight, woke at 2 o'clock and worked in his study until 5 am. He then went back to sleep until 7 am.

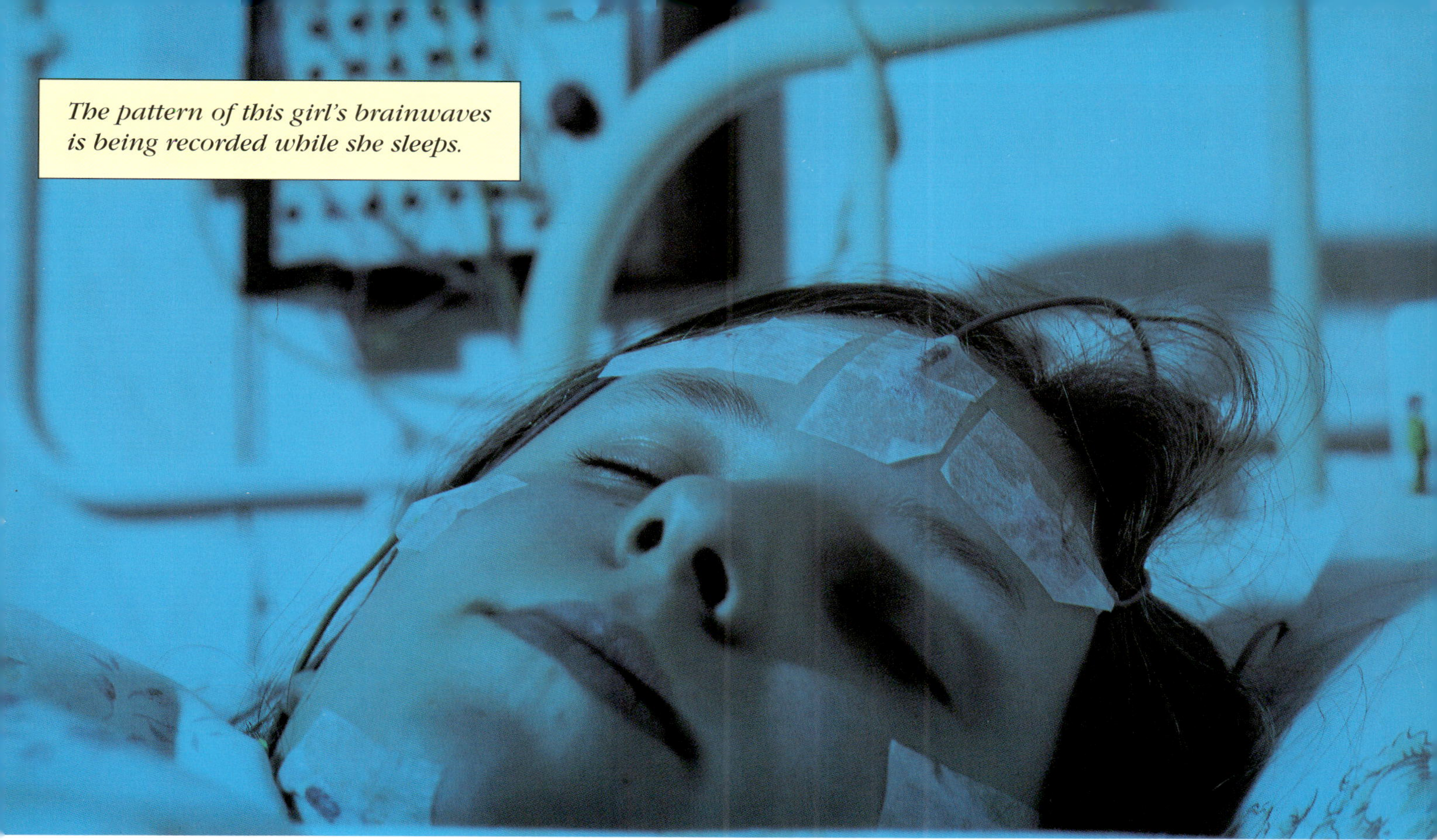

The pattern of this girl's brainwaves is being recorded while she sleeps.

Winston Churchill, the English prime minister who led Britain through World War II, worked until 3 or 4 o'clock in the morning and was up again at 8 am, but he usually had a two-hour afternoon nap.

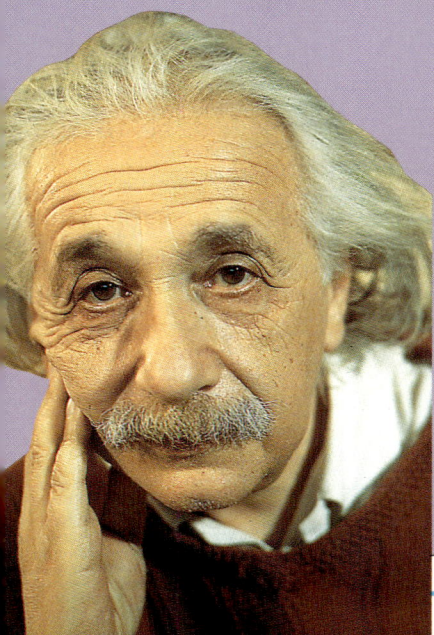

Albert Einstein, the German physicist who worked out the Theory of Relativity and the famous equation $E = mc^2$, was just the opposite. He spent ten hours a night asleep in bed.

Studying people's brainwaves while they sleep can provide more clues about how much sleep we need. The brainwaves of a sleeper who is really tired follow a different pattern from a normal sleeper.

After Randy Gardener had finished his record-breaking 11 days without sleep (look back at the case study on page 5), he slept for 15 hours and spent much of that time in deep Slow Wave Sleep.

Over the next few nights, he caught up on all the Slow Wave Sleep he'd missed during his 11 nights of staying awake. Randy also caught up on about half of the REM sleep that he'd missed. His brain didn't bother to catch up on the lighter stages of sleep. Other people who have gone without sleep show exactly the same sleeping pattern afterwards.

There is strong evidence that human beings need Slow Wave Sleep and REM sleep more than the lighter forms of sleep. Each night, shortly after you sink into deep Slow Wave Sleep, a gland in your brain called the pituitary gland releases a chemical called growth hormone. This chemical travels around your body and seems to act as a messenger, giving instructions to many different body cells. In children it triggers cells to grow, but it seems to be essential to the health of adults, too.

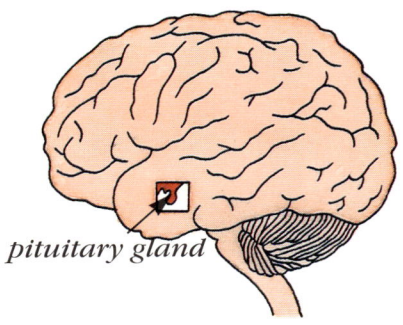

pituitary gland

Scientists have recorded the brainwaves of people who sleep for shorter than normal periods. They found that these people drop into Slow Wave Sleep as soon as they go to sleep. They actually spend the same amount of time in deep sleep as people who sleep for ten hours a night, and only miss out on the lighter stages of sleep.

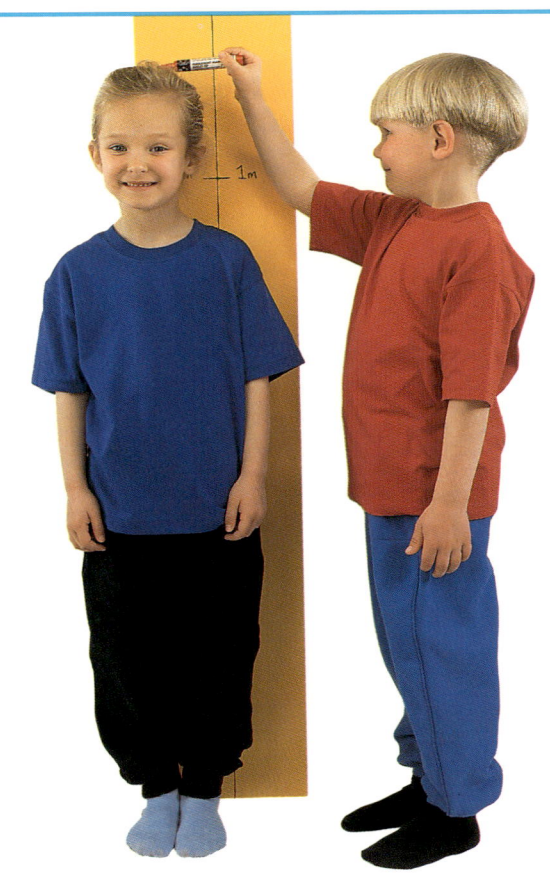

While we sleep, the brain releases a chemical that stimulates the body to grow, but this doesn't mean children who sleep the longest grow the fastest.

In young animals, the patterns of brainwaves during sleep are slightly different. Babies and children spend more time in REM sleep, the stage of sleep when people have their most vivid dreams. Newborn human babies have about eight hours of REM sleep a day. By their first birthday, this has dropped to about four hours, and it continues to decrease until, by the age of ten, children spend about as much of their sleep time in REM sleep as adults do.

Some scientists have suggested that REM sleep may be very important to the brain when it is growing and learning fast. This may be why young children sleep for longer and have more REM sleep than adults. Another suggestion is that the extra sleep young children have may be nature's way of allowing their parents some time to themselves.

Case study

In 1985, scientists at Loughborough University decided to find out if people could learn to live with less sleep. They chose six men and six women in their mid-twenties who normally slept for about eight hours a night. During the six-week experiment, six of the twelve volunteers continued to sleep normally, while the other six gradually reduced the amount they slept to six hours a night.

Throughout the experiment, people from both groups were given psychological tests to see how sleepy they were and how well they could work and concentrate. Their brain waves were also recorded.

The scientists found that there was really no difference between the two groups. The six people who had cut down their sleeping to six hours a night performed just as well as those who'd stayed asleep for eight hours. They felt fine too and most thought that they would probably try to keep to the routine of sleeping for only six hours because it would give them more time to do things.

The body's clock

Most of us wake up in the morning and go to sleep at night. This isn't just a habit we get into. There is a clock inside the body that helps it keep to this routine.

As bedtime approaches, your brain releases a chemical that signals to your kidneys to stop removing so much water from your blood. This means that your kidneys produce less urine so you don't need to get up in the night to go to the toilet.

These and many other body changes seem to happen in order to help people to feel sleepy at the right time, wake up at the right time and have a good night's sleep in between. But what is the right time? People's body clocks seem to be set differently.

In 1976 scientists at Loughborough University recorded the body temperature changes in a large number of people throughout the day. They found that the evening rise in temperature happened about an hour later in people who preferred to stay up at night and get up late in the morning.

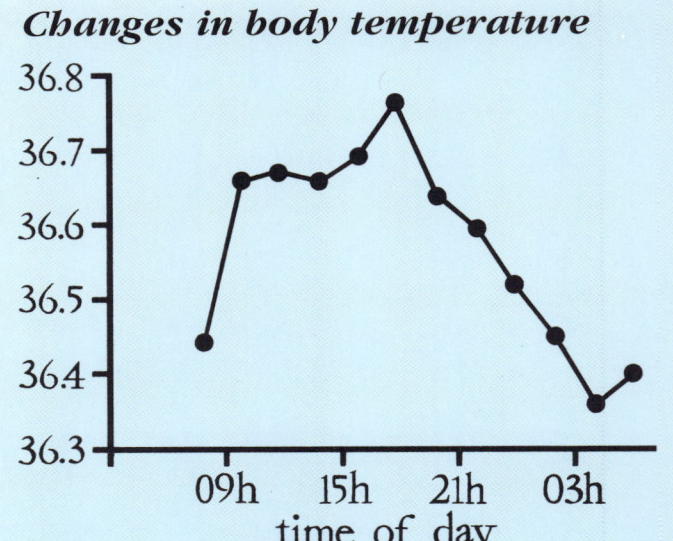

Changes in body temperature

time of day

The body's normal temperature is about 37 degrees centigrade, but this changes by up to half a degree throughout the day. Most people are warmest in the early evening, a few hours before bedtime, and coldest in the early morning, a few hours before they wake up. As wake-up time approaches, the body warms up the brain ready for the day.

For hundreds of thousands of years, humans have allowed their body clocks to control their daily habits. In recent times, things have changed. The invention of artificial light has meant that people can continue to work and play after dark and long after their body clocks say 'bedtime'. The invention of the jet aircraft has meant that people can travel to places where it is daytime when their body clocks are saying that it should be dark outside and time to sleep.

Floodlighting allows this baseball game to be played after dark.

Today, about six per cent of the world's population goes to work when everyone else is asleep. Workers on night shifts have to be alert and perhaps make important decisions at a time when their body clocks are telling them to sleep. Research has shown that this makes life difficult for the workers. Studies of night workers in Sweden showed that they didn't really sleep well during the day and still felt tired after they had woken up. They often felt so sleepy that they couldn't help dropping off to sleep, even when they were supposed to be working.

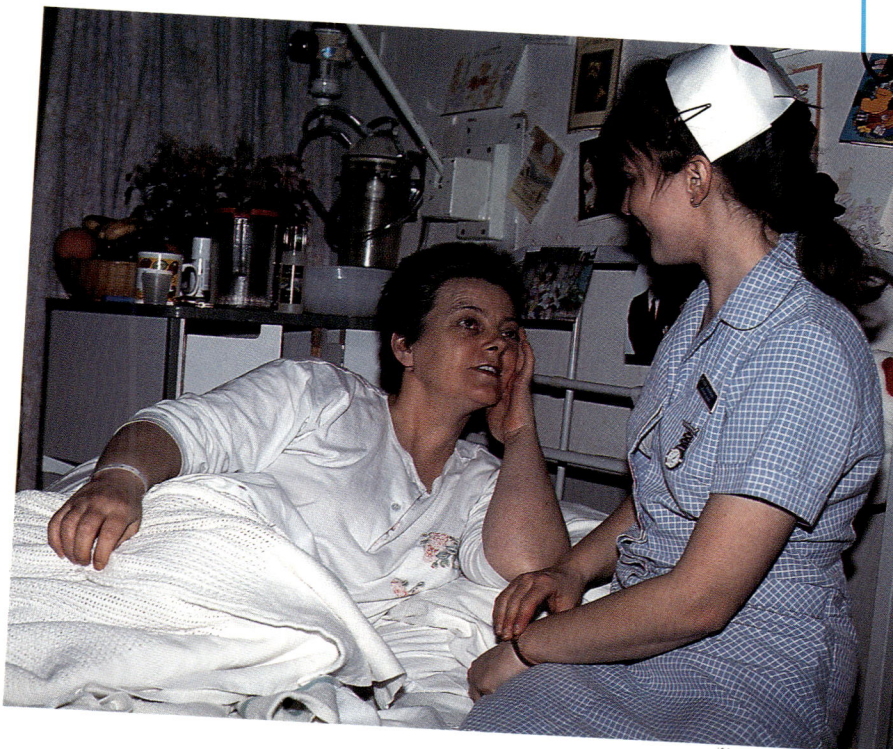

The night shift at a busy hospital. The staff have to be ready to come to the aid of a patient at any time throughout the night.

Case study: Linda Page

Linda Page worked for nine years as a stewardess on British Airways' transcontinental flights. Her body had to cope with shift work as well as with changing time zones. 'Your body gets very confused,' she explains. 'It's best to change your watch to the local time and try to forget what time it is where you've come from. Sometimes you have to catch up on your sleep by getting a couple of hours in the afternoon, but it's generally best to sleep at night when everyone else does. Otherwise, being awake in the middle of the night is the most depressing thing you can imagine.'

What sleep is and isn't

When people need surgery, they are often given drugs called anaesthetics to make them unconscious. Because they are unconscious, they don't feel pain during the operation and they don't remember anything about the operation afterwards. The doctor who gives the anaesthetic often says: 'I'm going to put you to sleep, now,' but patients aren't really asleep during operations. They can't wake up or move, and when they 'come round' from the anaesthetic they feel that no time has passed. It's quite a different experience from waking up from sleep.

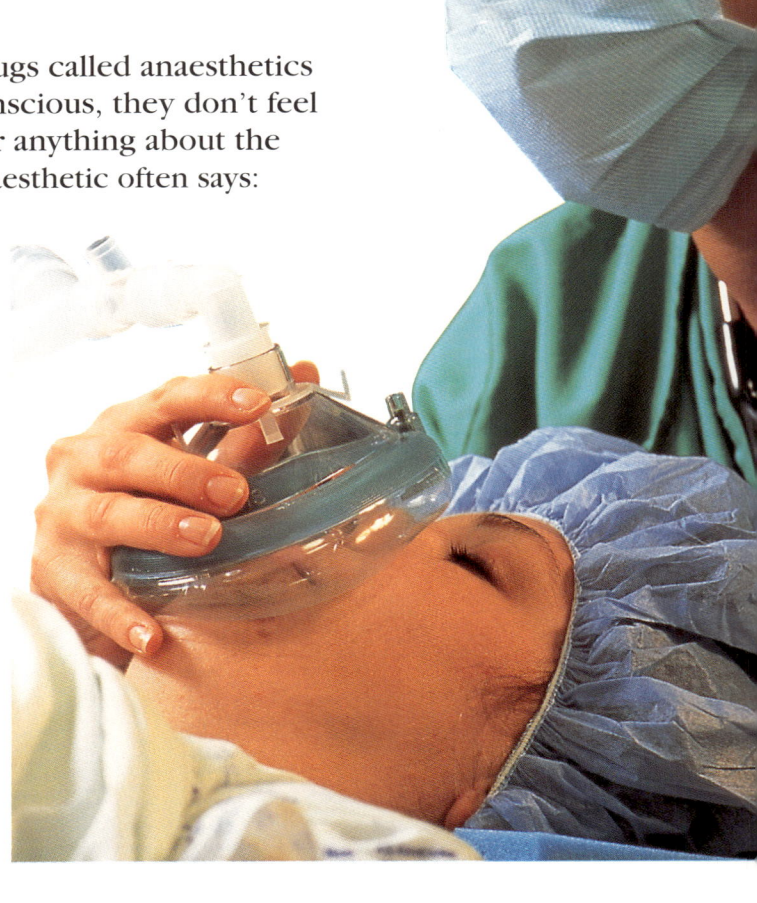

Comparing sleep to other states of consciousness has helped scientists to form a better idea of what sleep is. It is obvious that being asleep is different from being awake. When you sleep, you aren't conscious of what is going on around you. But you aren't exactly unconscious either, because things like a loud noise, a strange smell, a bright light, or a painful shove can wake you up. It's as if some part of your brain stays awake keeping watch so it can wake you up if there's something you need to wake up for.

When people are in a deep, hypnotic trance, they often let the hypnotist guide their feelings and actions. They appear to imagine the things that the hypnotist talks about and even act them out. It may seem as if they are in a dream but it is nothing like a dream. Dreams are formed inside the dreamer's mind and they are never acted out by the body because signals from the brain don't reach the muscles during a dream.

Many people enjoy watching and taking part in stage hypnotism.

Medical hypnotism

Hypnotists often say to people they are trying to hypnotize: 'You are beginning to feel very sleepy,' but according to Dr Malcolm Calder, they are not asleep. Dr Calder has been hypnotized several times. He is a G.P. who trained to become a hypnotist, so that he could use hypnosis to treat patients.

'The first time I was hypnotized, I didn't really notice any change,' he says. 'It felt so ordinary. People who are in a hypnotic trance are perfectly aware of what is going on around them. They can also remember having been in the trance, unless the hypnotist has suggested to them to forget what happened while they were hypnotized.'

Dr Calder has found that hypnosis has helped some of his patients who have trouble getting to sleep at night. 'It helps them learn to relax and stop thinking about things that are bothering them.' Dr Calder believes that it's much better than sleeping pills.

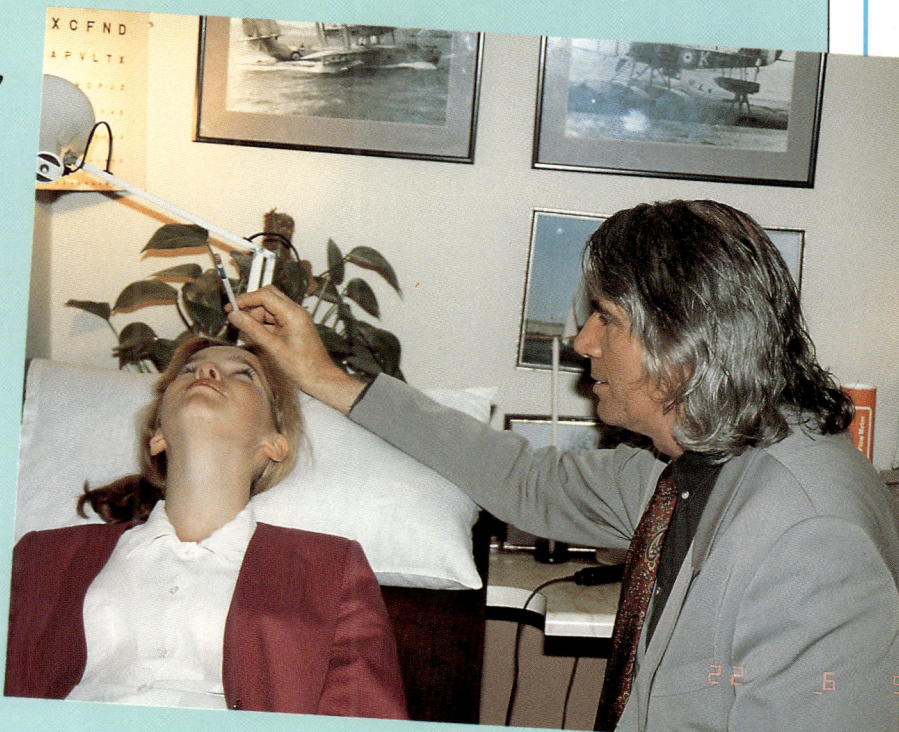

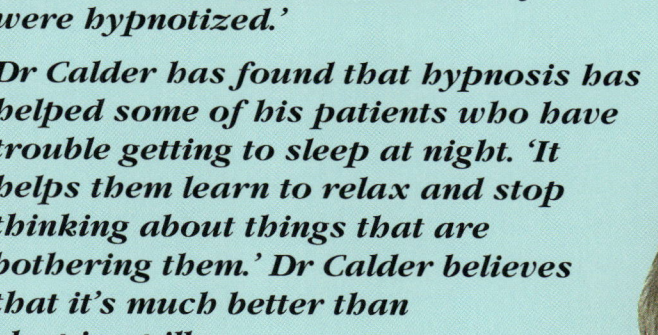

If a person wants to be hypnotized, it is usually not difficult for them to go into a trance.

If your brain is injured or isn't supplied with enough oxygen, it may not be able to work well enough to keep you conscious. In these cases people will say you have been 'knocked out' or 'have fainted'. People with an illness called epilepsy may lose consciousness every so often when the work of some of their brain cells becomes unco-ordinated. None of these kinds of unconsciousness are anything like sleep, but as people recover from these problems, they often sleep for longer than usual. The brain may need this extra sleep in order to heal.

I can't help it!

When you're awake, you are in control of your body, but when you go to sleep, you give up that control. It's rather like shutting your eyes and clicking a switch that sets your body onto 'automatic', so that you can have a rest and do some dreaming. This automatic control system works very well in most people most of the time. When it doesn't, it can be quite distressing.

In Shakespeare's play Macbeth, *Lady Macbeth walks in her sleep when her mind is troubled. In children though, sleepwalking doesn't seem to be linked with any problem; it just happens.*

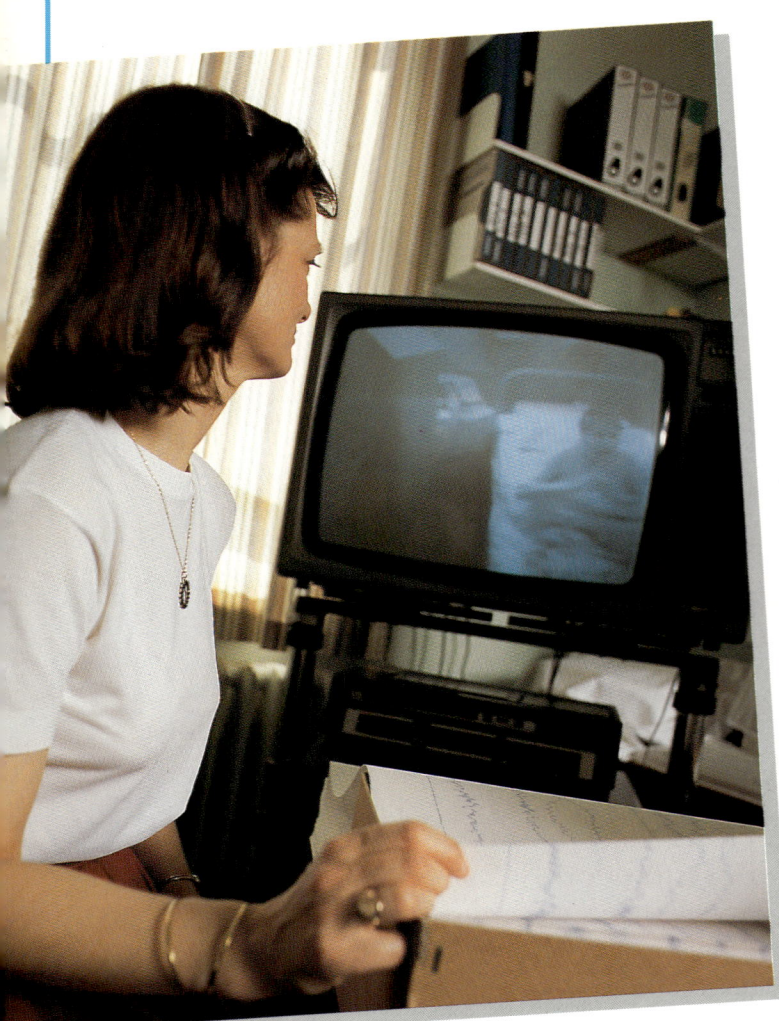

Quite a few children walk in their sleep. They get up in the night and start doing things, sometimes quite complicated things. Their eyes are open and it is often difficult at first to tell if they are awake or asleep.

Sleepwalking is quite common in children. Brainwave recordings show that, just before children begin to sleepwalk, they are in deep Slow Wave Sleep. Then suddenly, the pattern changes and becomes very similar to the brainwaves of an awake person. It is as if the brain has woken up and left the child deeply asleep.

Sleepwalking can be worrying, but part of the child's brain is awake and that usually works to keep the body out of danger. After a few minutes, the sleepwalker will either wake up completely or go to sleep completely. Children usually grow out of sleepwalking. Perhaps some children's automatic control system for sleeping needs a bit more practice to get it perfectly right.

The Nightmare *by* Henry Fuseli (1741-1825). *What causes bad dreams? Our daytime worries? The wrong kind of food too close to bedtime? Why we have nightmares is just as much of a mystery as why we dream at all.*

Most people have bad dreams at some time in their lives. Some people wake up in the night feeling very frightened or terribly sad without knowing why. Since no one understands dreaming, no one knows why these things happen. Most people go to sleep again afterwards and wake up in the morning feeling fine again.

Learning how to control when you go to the toilet is part of growing from a baby into a child, but when you go to sleep, that control must be taken over by the body's automatic control system. Most children need to wear a nappy at

night long after they have given up wearing one during the day. The automatic control system takes a little longer to learn this control.

In some children it takes longer than others. About one in twenty children starting school still wet the bed occasionally. Many are taken to the doctor to find out what is 'wrong' with them. The doctors hardly ever find anything wrong. It is normal for some children's bodies to take longer to learn this control, but doctors do have ways of helping children to stop wetting the bed.

Problems and potions

Almost everyone has trouble sleeping, or 'insomnia' at some time and it isn't just a problem of people living today. A thousand years ago, a person might have visited the local wise woman for help. In those days the patients might have been given some herbs to smell or to make into a tea and been advised to repeat a special incantation, or chant, to help them feel sleepy. Sometimes their sleep improved, sometimes it didn't.

Today people who can't sleep might try a herbal remedy or visit their doctor to ask for some sleeping tablets. Sometimes their sleep improves, sometimes it doesn't. Most doctors believe that taking sleeping tablets often does more harm than good.

Sleep scientists have learned a few things that might help people who have trouble sleeping, though. First of all, not being able to sleep is not always a problem. If you are worried or excited about something, it is normal to lie awake thinking about it.

This ancient Greek sculpture shows Aesculapius, the god of medicine, mixing a potion for his patient who is lying on a couch. Inscriptions on the god's temples of healing advise that rest is part of the prescription for good health.

Who can get to sleep at their normal bedtime on Christmas Eve? If you go to sleep later than usual, your brain will make the best of the sleep you do get by spending more time in deep Slow Wave Sleep. You can often catch up on your missed sleep during the next night.

If you have trouble getting to sleep every night, it may still not be a problem. Do you feel sleepy during the daytime? If you don't, perhaps you just don't need much sleep.

Most cultures have centuries' old remedies for sleeping problems.

Case study: John Leadley

Being sleepy during the day is a problem because it stops people working well and enjoying life. For 15 years, John Leadley had this problem. He would sleep for eleven hours, but an hour after waking up, he would be dropping off again. Doctors discovered that John had a condition called 'sleep apnoea'.

People with John's problem don't have a proper night's sleep because of a problem with their breathing. Every time they begin to sink into a deep sleep, the muscles of the throat relax and block the windpipe. This wakes them up enough to allow them to breathe again. The only way they can keep breathing is to spend the whole night sleeping very lightly.

John now goes to sleep wearing a mask connected to an air pump to help with his breathing and says that it has solved the problem. 'I'm a new man. I have a normal night's sleep now, and feel really awake during the day. For the first time I am able to enjoy playing with my grandchildren.'

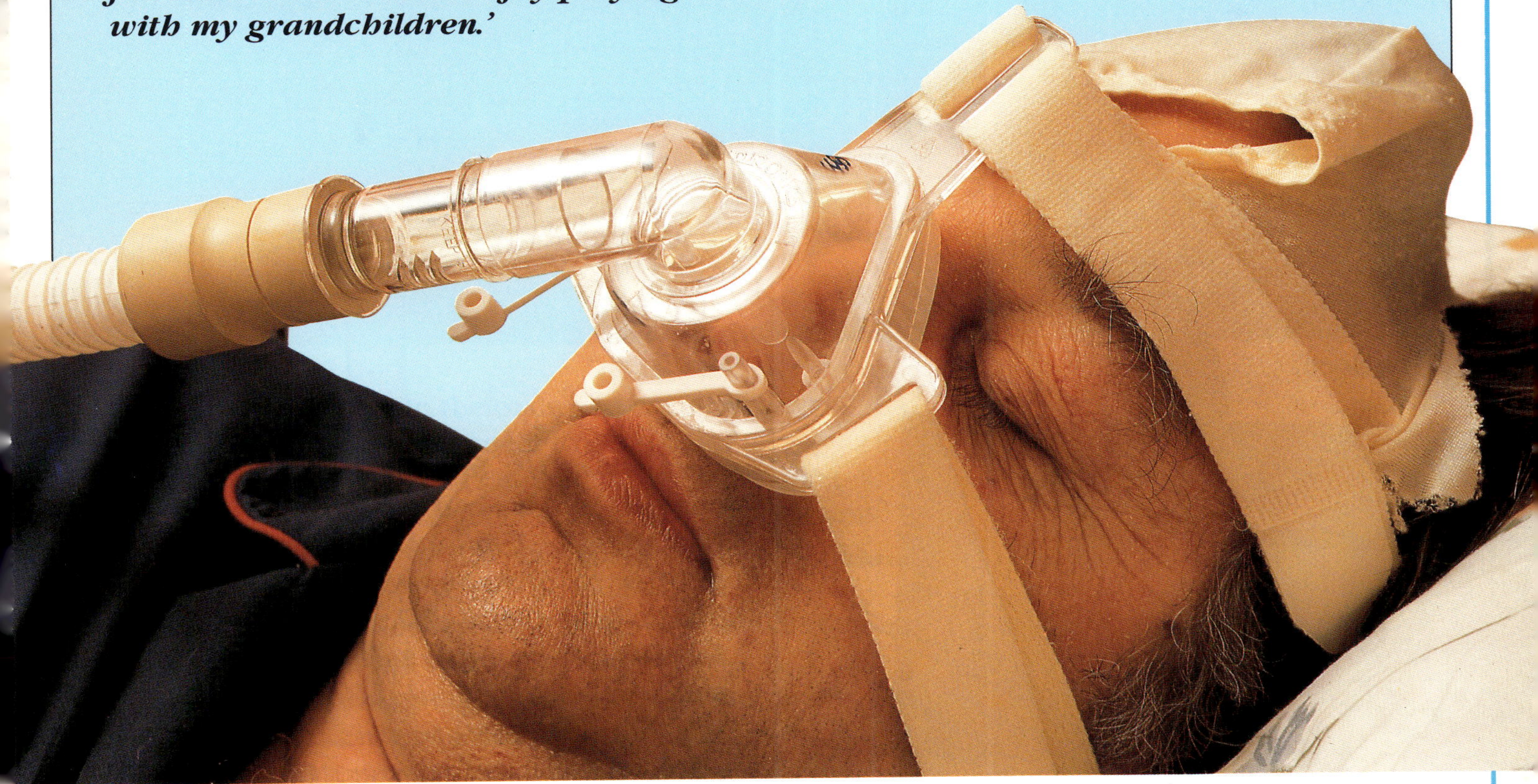

Being able to have a good night's sleep solves so many problems. Unfortunately, for the many people who have trouble sleeping, what sleep is, and how we get to sleep is still a mystery. Until we know more, today's doctors and chemists can't do much more than the wise women of ancient times.

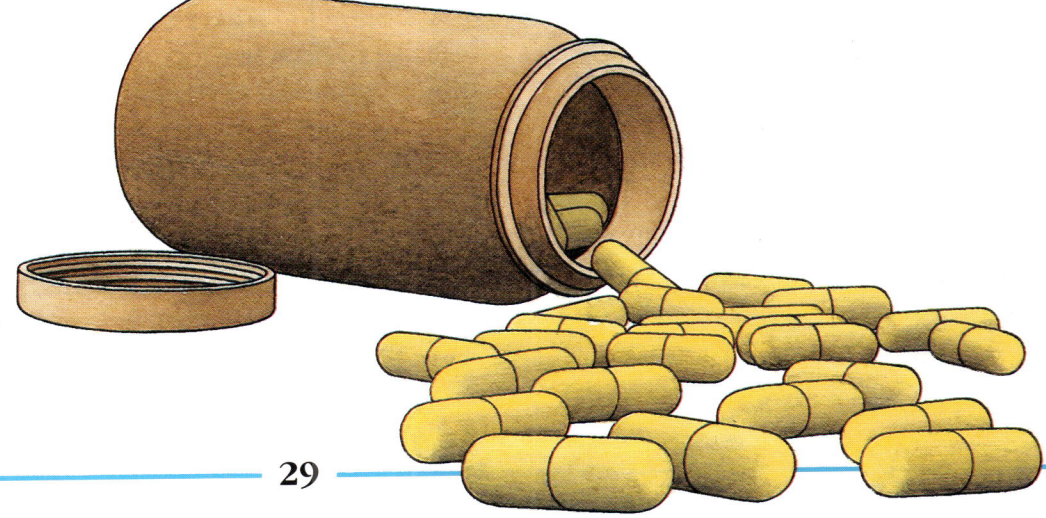